Let Freedom Ring

The Trail of Tears, 1838

by Laura Purdie Salas

Consultant:
Jack D. Baker
President
Trail of Tears Association
Little Rock, Arkansas

Bridgestone Books
an imprint of Capstone Press
Mankato, Minnesota

Bridgestone Books are published by Capstone Press
151 Good Counsel Drive, P.O. Box 669, Mankato, Minnesota 56002
http://www.capstone-press.com

Library of Congress Cataloging-in-Publication Data
Salas, Laura Purdie.
   The Trail of Tears, 1838 / by Laura Purdie Salas.
   p. cm. — (Let freedom ring)
   Summary: Discusses events leading up to the removal of the Cherokee from their homelands, hardships faced on the Trail of Tears, challenges of the new territory in Oklahoma, and the Cherokee nation today.
   Includes bibliographical references and index.
   ISBN 0-7368-1559-7 (hardcover)
   1. Trail of Tears, 1838—Juvenile literature. 2. Cherokee Indians—History—19th century—Juvenile literature. 3. Cherokee Indians—Relocation—Juvenile literature.
4. United States. Act to Provide for an Exchange of Lands with the Indians Residing in any of the States or Territories, and for Their Removal West of the River Mississippi. [1. Trail of Tears, 1838. 2. Cherokee Indians—History. 3. Indians of North America—Southern States—History.]
I. Title. II. Series.
E99.C5 S35 2003
973.04'975—dc21   2002008633

Editorial Credits
Carrie Braulick, editor; Kia Adams, series designer; Juliette Peters, book designer; Angi Gahler, illustrator; Kelly Garvin, photo researcher; Karen Risch, product planning editor

Photo Credits
Archives and Manuscripts Division of the Oklahoma Historical Society, 35, 36
Guthrie Studios/John Guthrie, 5
Max Standley/courtesy R. Michelson Galleries, cover
North Wind Picture Archives, 6, 9, 10, 12, 19, 21, 25
Oklahoma Historical Society, 32
San Jacinto Museum of History, 26
Stock Montage, Inc., 15, 23, 43; The Newberry Library, 16
Unicorn Stock Photos/D & I MacDonald, 39
Visuals Unlimited/David Sieren, cover (inset), 41
Woolaroc Museum, 29

1   2   3   4   5   6   08   07   06   05   04   03

Table of Contents

Chapter One

Settlers and the Cherokee

After the Revolutionary War (1775–1783) ended, the United States claimed a large area of North American land. The Cherokee were one group of American Indians already living in parts of this land. As U.S. settlers wanted more land, the Cherokee gave up parts of their land in various treaties.

In October 1838, about 12,000 Cherokee Indians began a journey westward. The Cherokee did not look forward to moving. The U.S. government was forcing them from their homeland to make more room for U.S. settlers. The government had set aside an area of land for the Cherokee and other Indians called Indian Territory. The Cherokee did not have the supplies necessary for their journey of about 1,000 miles (1,600 kilometers). They traveled through snowy

About 12,000 Cherokee moved west to Indian Territory after the U.S. government passed a law removing them from their homeland in 1830.

weather with no adequate shelter. Some did not have warm clothing. Many Cherokee became sick. Thousands of Cherokee died during the journey. The trip became known as the Trail of Tears.

Living in Peace

Hundreds of years ago, the Cherokee were the largest and most powerful Indian nation in the southern part of North America. They lived in the areas that are now Georgia, Tennessee, North Carolina, South Carolina, and Alabama. They hunted in parts of land that became Virginia, West Virginia, and Kentucky. The total land area they occupied was about 135,000 square miles (350,000 square kilometers).

Hernando de Soto explored North America in 1540. He was one of the first Europeans to meet American Indians.

Each Cherokee village had its own leaders. These leaders included peace chiefs and war chiefs. A council house was located in the center of each village. Members of the village met at the council house for ceremonies and important discussions.

The Cherokee lived simple lives. Cherokee women grew corn, beans, and squash. The men hunted deer, bears, turkeys, rabbits, and other wildlife. Older Cherokee helped raise children.

Cultures Collide

In the 1500s, Europeans began exploring North America. In 1540, Spanish explorer Hernando de Soto was one of the first Europeans to meet the Cherokee. De Soto and his group of soldiers were searching for gold. They sometimes stayed with Indians as they traveled. De Soto and his soldiers often treated the Indians poorly. The Spanish believed the Indians knew where gold was hidden in North America, but refused to tell them.

In the 1600s, England, which later became Great Britain, established 13 colonies on the east coast of North America. In the early 1700s, many English settlers crossed the Atlantic Ocean to live in the colonies.

The Cherokee had a trading relationship with early English colonists. The colonists gave the Cherokee beads, farming tools, fabrics, and rifles in exchange for animal skins and furs. The colonists made hats and other clothing with the skins and furs.

By the mid-1700s, Great Britain's 13 colonies had become crowded. Many people wanted to live west of the Appalachian Mountains. These mountains bordered the colonies to the west, extending from the southern colonies north to Canada. Settlers believed they would have room to build and farm west of the mountains. But the mountains were difficult to travel over.

After a path called the Wilderness Road was built through the Appalachians, many settlers traveled west of the mountains. The settlers called this area Kentucky. Kentucky had plentiful wildlife for settlers to hunt and land for them to grow crops. The Cherokee and other Indian nations who hunted in Kentucky did not want the settlers to take over their land. The settlers and Indians often fought with one another. The Indians thought they would lose their hunting land if settlers continued to move west.

Friends and Enemies in War

The Cherokee relationship with British settlers changed often. In 1754, the French and Indian War (1754–1763) started. During this war, France and Great Britain fought for control of land west of the Appalachians. At first, the Cherokee fought alongside the British. But after conflicts between the Cherokee and British settlers continued to occur in Kentucky, many Cherokee sided with the French.

American Indians traded with settlers throughout the 1600s and early 1700s. The Cherokee often gave furs to settlers in exchange for farming tools and other goods.

In 1763, France and Great Britain signed the Treaty of Paris to end the war. France gave up its claims to Canada and the territory between the Mississippi River and the Appalachian Mountains. Great Britain then claimed this land.

During the Revolutionary War, the colonists fought for freedom from British rule. Most of the Cherokee sided with Great Britain against the colonists. They were angry with the colonists for taking over their hunting land. In 1783, the

American Indians gave up much of their hunting land to U.S. settlers in treaties. After the late 1790s, the Cherokee could not obtain many goods by trading deerskins because they had given up so much of their hunting land.

colonists won their independence and formed the United States of America. The United States then claimed Great Britain's land west of the Appalachians. The United States considered the Cherokee defeated enemies. Many U.S. settlers moved westward after the Revolutionary War, causing even more conflicts between the settlers and the Cherokee.

Treaties

In 1785, the Cherokee signed the Treaty of Hopewell. It was the first treaty in which the Cherokee gave land to the United States. The U.S. government promised not to allow settlers to move onto Cherokee territory. But settlers ignored the treaty because they wanted more land.

The Cherokee continued to sign treaties with the United States, giving up parts of their land in most of them. Each time, the Cherokee hoped the settlers would be satisfied with the land they had received. But they never were. Settlers continued to ignore treaties and move onto Cherokee land. By 1819, Cherokee territory made up only about 17,000 square miles (44,000 square kilometers).

A New Way of Life

In the late 1700s, many settlers believed the Indians were uncivilized. Indians lived simply. They did not use advanced farming tools and methods as the settlers did. Some settlers thought the Indian way of life was inferior to their own.

The U.S. government wanted the Indians to live more like settlers. Government leaders thought this would end frontier fighting. The Cherokee hoped that becoming more like the settlers might stop the U.S. government from taking over Cherokee land.

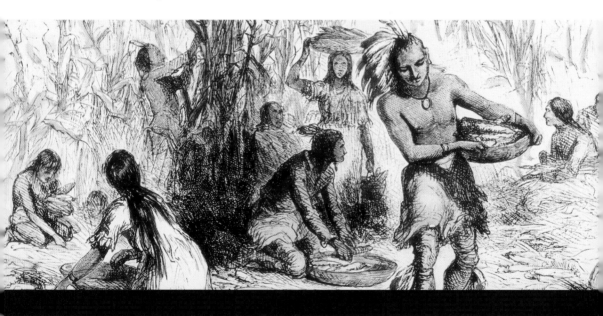

American Indians grew and harvested their food by hand instead of using advanced farming tools.

Thoughts on Civilization

". . . Now the thought of being compelled to remove [to] the other side of the Mississippi is dreadful to us . . . for we have, by the endeavor of our Father the President, become too much enlightened to throw aside the privileges of a civilized life . . ."

— A Cherokee Woman, June 30, 1818

In the early 1790s, the U.S. government sent settlers called agents to live with the Cherokee. The agents gave the Cherokee advanced farm tools and farming advice. Throughout the next several years, the Cherokee learned to farm crops. Many grew and harvested cotton. The Cherokee hunted less and raised more livestock. Religious teachers called missionaries taught the Cherokee about Christianity. This religion follows the life and teachings of Jesus Christ. Some Cherokee began to practice this religion instead of following their traditional beliefs.

Some Cherokee did not want to adopt the settlers' way of life. Instead, they chose to move west across the Mississippi River. This land was still a wilderness where they could practice their customs without interference from settlers.

Chapter Two

The Start of Indian Removal

Thomas Jefferson was U.S. president from 1801 to 1809. In 1803, the United States bought the Louisiana Territory from France. This land extended from the Mississippi River west to the Rocky Mountains and from the Gulf of Mexico north to Canada. To help solve problems between settlers and American Indians, Jefferson wanted to move the Indians to a part of the Louisiana Territory. Settlers called this area Indian Territory. It later became the state of Oklahoma.

Small Deals

The U.S. government wanted to give land west of the Mississippi River to the Indians in exchange for land the Indians already occupied.

Thomas Jefferson believed western expansion was important. He encouraged the purchase of the Louisiana Territory from France.

Government officials sometimes offered goods and other rewards to bribe Indian leaders into signing agreements. These Indian leaders did not always have the authority to sell the land. But they made deals anyway. Settlers then took over the land, and many Indians were forced to move.

In 1817 and 1819, the Cherokee gave up more of their eastern land in treaties with the United States. The treaties encouraged the Cherokee to move west of the Mississippi. But they also allowed some Cherokee to receive sections of land called

In 1828, the Cherokee elected John Ross as chief. Ross was an active leader throughout the next several years. He traveled to Washington, D.C., several times to express the Cherokee's opinion on policies to government leaders.

reservations in eastern states. These Cherokee would each receive 640 acres (259 hectares) and become residents of the state in which they lived. Some of these Cherokee became residents of North Carolina.

As a result of the treaties, some Cherokee moved west of the Mississippi to an area that later became Arkansas. But most Cherokee stayed on their remaining homeland. In 1819, Cherokee leaders notified the U.S. government that they would give no more land to settlers.

In 1827, the Cherokee created their own constitution and an official government system. In 1828, they elected John Ross as chief. They also formed the Cherokee Council. Members of the nation elected this group of leaders. Ross and the Cherokee Council made decisions for the entire Cherokee nation.

More Pressure

In 1828, Andrew Jackson was elected U.S. president. He wanted to pass the Indian Removal Act. This law would give the president authority to exchange U.S. western land with the Indians' eastern land.

That same year, settlers discovered gold on Cherokee land in Georgia. The Georgia government made it illegal for the Cherokee to dig for gold on their own land. Georgia claimed the Cherokee land and gave it to settlers. These actions broke agreements between the U.S. government and the Cherokee.

Georgia established other laws governing the Cherokee. Georgia officials would not allow the Cherokee Council to assemble. They did not treat the Cherokee fairly in the state's court system. Georgia created a police force called the Georgia Guard to enforce laws relating to Indians. Many settlers treated the Cherokee poorly. Georgia citizens demanded that the U.S. government force the Cherokee to move.

Resisting Laws

As problems grew, small groups of Cherokee moved west. But most Cherokee refused to move. Many

Cherokee did not believe Georgia had the right to govern them. They wanted to fight the laws in the U.S. court system. They thought they could win a case.

The Cherokee had other reasons for refusing to move. They did not believe the land in Indian Territory had enough resources for them to survive. The Cherokee did not want to create problems with the Indian nations already there. Some wealthy Cherokee feared they would not be able to make as much money after they moved west.

Settlers discovered gold on Cherokee land in 1828. They soon passed a series of laws restricting the rights of the Cherokee.

Chapter Three

Indian Removal Becomes Law

In May 1830, Congress passed the Indian Removal Act by one vote. This law called for 100,000 Indians to move west, including members of the Cherokee, Choctaw, Creek, Chickasaw, and Seminole nations. President Jackson was determined to follow through with Indian removal.

In September 1830, Jackson's officials bribed some Choctaw chiefs. The Choctaw leaders then signed a treaty giving up all their land east of the Mississippi River. The Choctaw moved west to Indian Territory. Many Creek, Chickasaw, and Seminole soon followed. The Cherokee were the last tribe left in Georgia and the surrounding area.

Andrew Jackson supported the Indian Removal Act. He made plans to move the Indians soon after the law passed.

In Jackson's Words

"It gives me pleasure to announce to Congress that the benevolent policy of the Government . . . in relation to the removal of the Indians beyond the white settlements is approaching a happy consummation . . ."

"What good man would prefer a country covered with forests and ranged by a few thousand savages to our extensive Republic . . . occupied by more than 12,000,000 happy people, and filled with all the blessings of liberty, civilization, and religion?"

—Parts of Andrew Jackson's State of the Union Address, December 6, 1830

A Meaningless Victory

The Cherokee challenged Georgia's laws in the court system. In 1831, the U.S. Supreme Court ruled that the Cherokee did not have the right to challenge Georgia in court.

In 1825, a missionary named Samuel Worcester had moved from Boston to Cherokee territory to teach Christianity to the Cherokee. In 1831, Worcester broke a Georgia law that required him to officially recognize Georgia's authority. The Georgia Guard arrested him.

Worcester had the authority to file a case against Georgia because he was a U.S. citizen. In 1832, Worcester won the case. The U.S. Supreme Court recognized the Cherokee as an independent nation. It ruled that Georgia could not make laws governing the Cherokee or give away Cherokee land to settlers. But Georgia refused to follow the ruling. President Jackson also ignored the Supreme Court's ruling.

The Treaty of New Echota

In 1835, a small group of Cherokee signed the Treaty of New Echota. By signing this treaty, the group agreed to

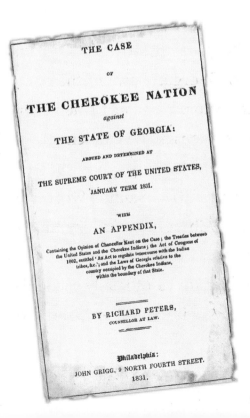

THE CASE

OF

THE CHEROKEE NATION

against

THE STATE OF GEORGIA:

ARGUED AND DETERMINED AT

THE SUPREME COURT OF THE UNITED STATES,

JANUARY TERM 1831.

WITH

AN APPENDIX,

Containing the Opinion of Chancellor Kent on the Case ; the Treaties between the United States and the Cherokee Indians ; the Act of Congress of 1802, entitled ' An Act to regulate intercourse with the Indian tribes, &c.'; and the Laws of Georgia relative to the country occupied by the Cherokee Indians, within the boundary of that State.

BY RICHARD PETERS,

COUNSELLOR AT LAW.

Philadelphia:

JOHN GRIGG, 9 NORTH FOURTH STREET.

1831.

In 1831, the Cherokee presented their case against Georgia to the Supreme Court. This photo shows the title page of the Supreme Court's ruling.

the Indian Removal Act. The treaty signers did not have authority to sign the treaty. But Jackson approved the treaty anyway. The men who signed the treaty led small groups of Cherokee to Indian Territory. They chose the best available land for their homes.

Chief Ross traveled to Washington, D.C. He presented a petition with the names of almost 16,000 Cherokee who opposed the treaty. The U.S. government ignored the petition. According to the Indian Removal Act, the Cherokee needed to leave their land by May 1838.

The Roundup Begins

Since most Cherokee disagreed with the treaty, many remained in their homeland until they were forced to leave. By 1837, Jackson's term as president had ended. President Martin Van Buren thought the Cherokee might fight against the soldiers who were trying to remove them. He sent General John E. Wool to take away the Cherokee's weapons. Wool resigned from the army because he felt the Cherokee were being treated unfairly.

General Winfield Scott replaced Wool. Scott wanted to follow the president's orders. He began the roundup on May 23, 1838. He sent more than 7,000 soldiers onto Cherokee land. They herded the Cherokee into 31 forts in Georgia, Alabama, Tennessee, and North Carolina. Most people had to leave everything behind. Some settlers moved into Cherokee homes even before the owners were off the property.

About 1,400 Cherokee escaped the roundup. Some Cherokee escaped to wilderness areas and hid from soldiers. Others avoided the roundup because they had received reservations in the treaties of 1817 and 1819. These Cherokee had become residents of North Carolina. State officials agreed to let these Cherokee stay in their homeland.

Winfield Scott was in charge of the Cherokee roundup. He persuaded the soldiers to treat the Cherokee with respect and kindness, although soldiers still mistreated many Cherokee.

Cherokee Supporters

The Cherokee had many supporters. One of these supporters was former President John Quincy Adams. Other famous supporters were U.S. politicians Davy Crockett and Sam Houston. Crockett and Houston were members of Congress and had spent time living with the Cherokee. Houston (pictured below) also had served as governor of Tennessee. He had been a schoolmate of John Ross.

Other Americans who supported the Cherokee knew them as good friends and neighbors. They thought it was wrong to force the Cherokee to move. Many Americans wrote protest letters to the government. But the government ignored the letters.

The Prison Camps

The Cherokee stayed at the forts for a short time. Soldiers then moved the Cherokee from the forts to prison camps in Alabama and Tennessee.

The soldiers often abused the Cherokee at these prisons. The Cherokee did not receive proper medical treatment. They did not have enough water or food. They had no shelter from harsh weather. Many Cherokee died in the prisons.

A New Plan

Chief Ross had been in Washington, D.C., when the soldiers rounded up the Cherokee. After Ross returned to Cherokee territory, he learned about the terrible conditions at the prison camps. Ross talked to General Scott. He wanted the Cherokee to arrange their own journey west.

General Scott and the U.S. government agreed to Ross' plan. The Cherokee began preparing for their journey. They thought the trip to their new home would take 80 days.

Chapter Four

The Move West

On October 1, 1838, about 12,000 Cherokee gathered to begin their journey of 600 to 1,200 miles (966 to 1,931 kilometers). Most Cherokee were along the Hiwassee River in Tennessee. Others were at camps in southern Tennessee and in Alabama. Many Cherokee were weak or sick from months in prison camps. Chief Ross said a short prayer to the crowd, and the long trek began.

Conditions on the Trail

The Cherokee divided into 13 groups for the journey. They traveled in various ways. Most people walked. Covered wagons carried supplies and the sickest and oldest people. Some Cherokee rode horses or mules.

The journey of the Cherokee to Indian Territory lasted several months longer than they had expected.

Each morning, the Cherokee ate a small breakfast, packed their wagons, and began walking. Hunters sometimes left the trail on horseback to kill animals for food. Most Cherokee walked all day, many without shoes. Many walked through cold weather conditions without warm clothing. The Cherokee sometimes needed to cross private land or use ferries to cross rivers. Settlers often charged the Cherokee tolls to pass through these areas. Many people charged the Cherokee much more money than normal.

After the Cherokee stopped each day, they built fires and cooked dinner. They often ate ground corn and any animals the hunters had killed. Most Cherokee slept in tents, but few Cherokee had enough supplies to keep them warm at night.

The Cherokee's march continued through a rainy, muddy fall and a cold winter. The last group reached Indian Territory in March 1839. The journey had taken nearly six months. Most Cherokee had

Trail of Tears Routes

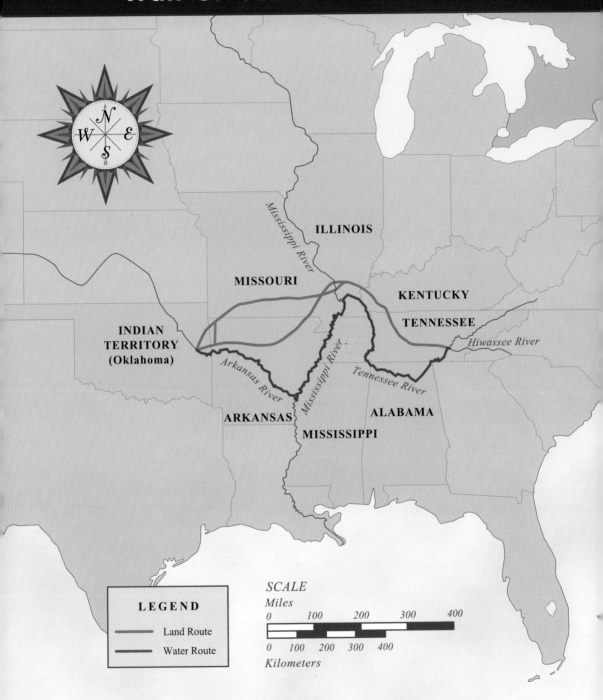

ILLINOIS

MISSOURI

KENTUCKY

TENNESSEE

Mississippi River

Hiwassee River

INDIAN
TERRITORY
(Oklahoma)

Arkansas River

Mississippi River

Tennessee River

ARKANSAS

ALABAMA

MISSISSIPPI

LEGEND

Land Route

Water Route

SCALE

Miles

0   100   200   300   400

0   100   200   300   400

Kilometers

traveled through present-day Kentucky, southern Illinois, and southern Missouri to reach Indian Territory. Others had turned south in Illinois and traveled through northern Arkansas to reach Indian Territory.

Many Deaths

Many history experts believe that as many as 4,000 Cherokee died as they traveled. Many died after becoming sick. Others died after being exposed to the cold weather conditions for long periods of time. The trail west was dotted with graves from start to finish.

The Cherokee took different routes on the Trail of Tears, but most arrived in Indian Territory in spring 1839.

Travel by Boat

Not all Cherokee traveled land routes to Indian Territory. In June 1838, U.S. soldiers divided about 2,400 Cherokee into three groups. The soldiers sent these groups aboard flatboats. These boats had flat bottoms and square sides.

The flatboats floated along the Tennessee River, Mississippi River, and Arkansas River to reach Indian Territory. The boats were crowded. Little clean drinking water was available. Travel was dangerous because a lack of rainfall made the water levels low. The flatboats ran into sandbars. Two of the groups had to leave their boats in Arkansas and walk to Indian Territory. People also got sick from the heat and dirty conditions. More than 200 Cherokee died.

The march was so brutal and so many died, that the Cherokee later called it Nunda'utsun'yi, or "The Place Where They Cried." The routes they took became known as the Trail of Tears.

Chapter Five

Arrival in Indian Territory

The Cherokee who arrived in Indian Territory had survived a harsh journey. But a whole new set of challenges awaited them as they settled in an unfamiliar land.

Obstacles to Settlement

Indians already lived in the territory. Some were Cherokee, and some belonged to other nations. The other Indian nations did not want more Cherokee there. The Cherokee already living there wanted to keep their own government.

The U.S. government had promised to provide food and supplies to the Cherokee after they arrived in Indian Territory. But the food often was spoiled. There were not enough supplies for the thousands of Cherokee in Indian Territory.

Soon after they arrived in Indian Territory, John Ross purchased this home for his daughter.

One Nation

Chief Ross wanted to unite the Cherokee who had most recently arrived in Indian Territory with the group that had arrived earlier. In 1839, the two groups agreed to join together to become the Cherokee Nation. The Cherokee worked to establish a working economy in Indian Territory. They built a capital city called Tahlequah. They built stores, a hotel, and a courthouse. They also built schools called seminaries. The Cherokee started a newspaper called the *Cherokee Advocate*. Some

In 1820, U.S. missionaries established this school in Indian Territory to teach American Indian children about Christianity.

Cherokee became wealthy by raising cattle or by producing salt, which people bought to preserve meat.

The Civil War

From 1846 to 1861, the Cherokee Nation enjoyed economic growth. The Civil War (1861–1865) then split their nation. Southern states had broken away from the United States to form their own country. These states were called the South, or the Confederate States of America. Some Cherokee supported the Confederacy. Other Cherokee supported the North, or the Union. Supporters of both sides destroyed each other's houses, barns, and fields. Many Cherokee were killed. After the Civil War, Chief Ross worked to reunite the Cherokee Nation.

By the 1880s, the Cherokee had once again become successful. They used railroads to trade goods with people in the eastern United States. The capital of Tahlequah became a well-known educational center.

By the 1900s, many settlers had moved into the area. In 1907, the U.S. government forced the Cherokee Nation to abandon its government and become part of the state of Oklahoma. Some Cherokee became state government leaders.

Chapter Six

Modern Cherokee

Today, some American Indians in the United States live on reservations. The U.S. government set aside these areas of land for use by American Indians. The U.S. government recognizes more than 550 Indian nations.

Three Cherokee Nations

Three main Cherokee nations live in the United States. The nations have separate governments, but they communicate regularly. About 300,000 Cherokee are members of the Cherokee Nation. Many of these Cherokee live in northeastern Oklahoma. Members are descendants of Cherokee who traveled on the Trail of Tears.

The United Keetoowah Band (UKB) of Cherokee Indians lives in the same area of Oklahoma as the Cherokee Nation. About 12,000 Cherokee are part of the UKB.

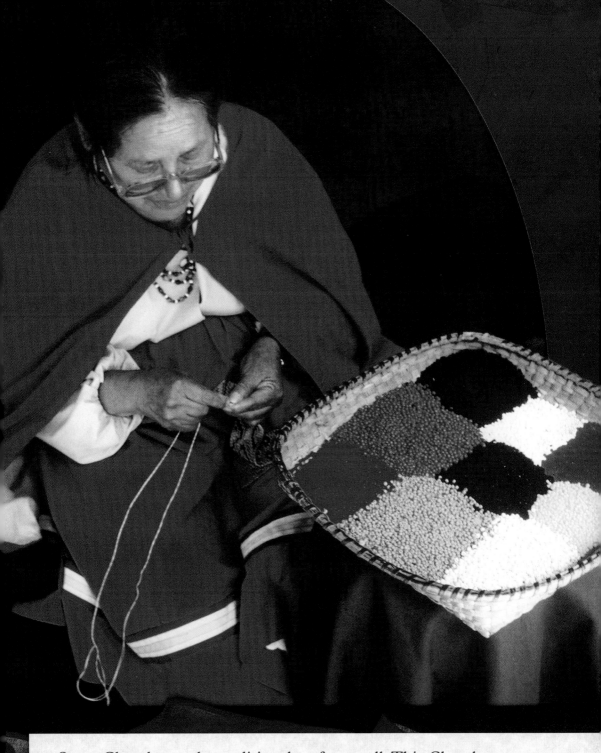

Some Cherokee make traditional crafts to sell. This Cherokee woman is beading.

The Eastern Band of Cherokee Indians also has about 12,000 people. This band lives on a reservation in North Carolina. Members of the Eastern Band of Cherokee Indians are descendants of Cherokee who avoided the Trail of Tears.

The Cherokee have customs similar to those of most Americans. Many work in large cities in business professions. Some are farmers or hold government positions.

Many Cherokee still celebrate their culture with traditional ceremonies and events. Some Cherokee continue to make baskets, pots, masks, and other traditional crafts.

Exploring the Trail of Tears

Several parks and other organizations have established places where visitors can learn more about the Trail of Tears. Some cities and states have sites to honor the people who died on the Trail of Tears.

In 1987, Congress made the Trail of Tears a National Historic Trail. People can drive along highways that closely follow the original trail or hike along parts of the trail. The trail serves as a reminder to people that many lives were lost as U.S. settlers moved across the western frontier.

The Legend of the Cherokee Rose

Cherokee sometimes tell the legend of the Cherokee Rose.
The story says many mothers cried on the hard march to
Indian Territory. A rose grew at every spot where a mother's
tear dropped to the ground. Today, the Cherokee Rose is
the official state flower of Georgia. It still grows along parts
of the Trail of Tears route.

TIMELINE

The American Revolution begins. The Cherokee fight on the side of the British.

Hernando de Soto meets the Cherokee.

| 1540 | 1754 | 1775 | 1785 |

The French and Indian War begins. The Cherokee fight for and then against the British in the war.

In the Treaty of Hopewell, the Cherokee give land to the United States. The U.S. government promises to protect the Cherokee land.

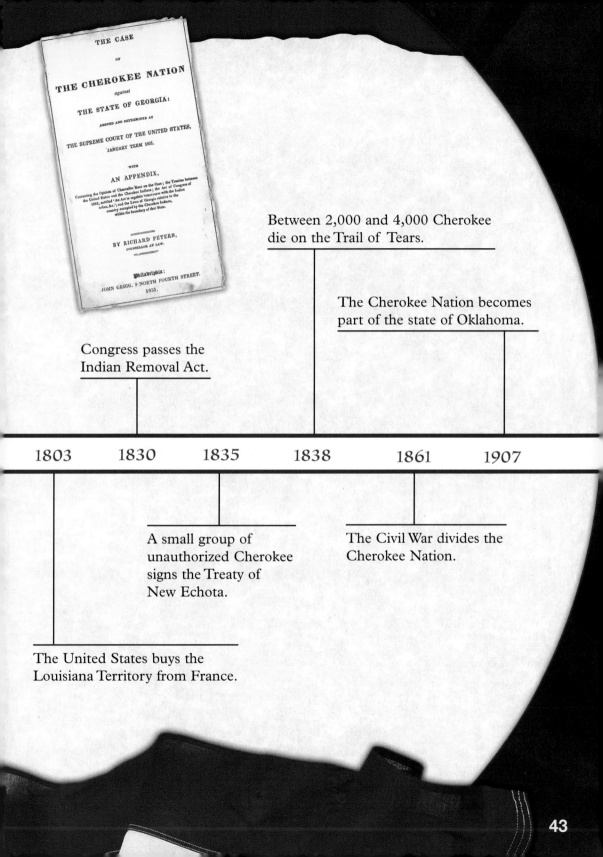

THE CASE
OF
THE CHEROKEE NATION
against
THE STATE OF GEORGIA:
ARGUED AND DETERMINED AT
THE SUPREME COURT OF THE UNITED STATES,
JANUARY TERM 1831.

WITH
AN APPENDIX,
Containing the Opinion of Chancellor Kent on the Case; the Treaties between the United States and the Cherokee Indians; the Act of Congress of 1802, entitled "An Act to regulate intercourse with the Indian tribes, &c."; and the Laws of Georgia relative to the country occupied by the Cherokee Indians, within the boundary of that State.

BY RICHARD PETERS,
COUNSELLOR AT LAW.

Philadelphia:
JOHN GRIGG, 9 NORTH FOURTH STREET.
1831.

Between 2,000 and 4,000 Cherokee
die on the Trail of Tears.

The Cherokee Nation becomes
part of the state of Oklahoma.

Congress passes the
Indian Removal Act.

| 1803 | 1830 | 1835 | 1838 | 1861 | 1907 |

A small group of
unauthorized Cherokee
signs the Treaty of
New Echota.

The Civil War divides the
Cherokee Nation.

The United States buys the
Louisiana Territory from France.

Glossary

authority (uh-THOR-uh-tee)—the right to do something or to tell other people what to do

bribe (BRIBE)—to give money or a gift to someone so the person will make an agreement

descendant (di-SEND-uhnt)—a person's child and the generations of a family born after that child

economy (i-KON-uh-mee)—the way a group manages its money, goods, and services

inferior (in-FIHR-ee-ur)—of lesser value than something else

livestock (LIVE-stok)—farm animals kept for use or profit

nation (NAY-shuhn)—a group of people who often live in the same area and speak the same language

petition (puh-TISH-uhn)—a written request signed by many people asking those in power to change their policy or actions

toll (TOHL)—a charge paid for using a ferry, highway, bridge, or tunnel

treaty (TREE-tee)—a formal agreement between two or more groups of people or nations

For Further Reading

Barrett, Tracy. *The Trail of Tears: An American Tragedy.* Cover to Cover Books. Logan, Iowa: Perfection Learning, 2000.

Bruchac, Joseph. *The Trail of Tears.* Step into Reading. New York: Random House, 2003.

Johnston, Tony. *Trail of Tears.* New York: Blue Sky Press, 1998.

Roop, Peter. *If You Lived with the Cherokee.* New York: Scholastic, 1998.

Todd, Anne M. *The Cherokee: An Independent Nation.* American Indian Nations. Mankato, Minn.: Bridgestone Books, 2003.

Places of Interest

Cherokee Heritage Center
P.O. Box 515
Tahlequah, OK 74465
This center is the site of the
Cherokee National Museum and
a rebuilt model of an ancient
Cherokee village.

Cherokee Trail of Tears Park
9th Street and Skyline Drive
Hopkinsville, KY 42241
This park has campsites that were
used by the Cherokee on the Trail
of Tears. Two Cherokee leaders
who died on the Trail of Tears are
buried here.

Museum of the Cherokee Indian
P.O. Box 1599
Cherokee, NC 28719
Exhibits and educational programs
at this museum teach visitors about
Cherokee history.

New Echota Historic Site
1211 Chatsworth Highway NE
Calhoun, GA 30701
This park features the restored
house of Samuel Worcester and the
rebuilt *Cherokee Phoenix* print shop.

Trail of Tears State Park
429 Moccasin Springs
Jackson, MO 63755
A monument marks the gravesite of
a Cherokee who died on the Trail
of Tears, and the park includes
2 miles (3.2 kilometers) of the
Trail of Tears route.

Internet Sites

Do you want to learn more about The Trail of Tears?
Visit the FACT HOUND at *http://www.facthound.com*

FACT HOUND can track down many sites to help you.
All the FACT HOUND sites are hand-selected
by Capstone Press editors. FACT HOUND will fetch the best,
most accurate information to answer your questions.

IT IS EASY! IT IS FUN!
1) Go to *http://www.facthound.com*
2) Type in: 0736815597
3) Click on "FETCH IT" and
    FACT HOUND will put you
    on the trail of several helpful links.

You can also search by subject or book title. So, relax
and let our pal FACT HOUND do the research for you!

Index